JAZZ FUNERAL

JAZZ FUNERAL

poems

Julie Kane

Story Line Press | *Pasadena, CA*

Jazz Funeral
Copyright © 2009, 2021 by Julie Kane
All Rights Reserved

ISBN 978-1-58654-064-7 (tradepaper)
  978-1-58654-078-4 (casebound)

The National Endowment for the Arts, the Los Angeles County Arts Commission, the Ahmanson Foundation, the Dwight Stuart Youth Fund, the Max Factor Family Foundation, the Pasadena Tournament of Roses Foundation, the Pasadena Arts & Culture Commission and the City of Pasadena Cultural Affairs Division, the City of Los Angeles Department of Cultural Affairs, the Audrey & Sydney Irmas Charitable Foundation, the Kinder Morgan Foundation, the Meta & George Rosenberg Foundation, the Allergan Foundation, the Riordan Foundation, Amazon Literary Partnership, and the Mara W. Breech Foundation partially support Red Hen Press.

Second Edition
Published by Story Line Press
an imprint of Red Hen Press
www.redhen.org

Acknowledgments

Grateful acknowledgment is made to the editors of the following publications, in which the listed poems appeared, sometimes in a slightly different form:

14 by 14: "Finale"; *The Antioch Review*: "Ode on Grimalkin Urns"; *The Book of Hopes and Dreams*, ed. Dee Rimbaud (Bluechrome, 2006): "15 March 2003"; *The Evansville Review*: "Rising and Falling"; *The Formalist*: "Used Book"; *Louisiana English Journal*: "The Terror of the Place"; *Mezzo Cammin*: "Cardinal," "The Killing Field," "Particle Physics," and "First Re-Entry, Post-Katrina"; *The New Laurel Review*: "A Hobo's Crown for Robert Borsodi"; *Poets USA*: "Player Piano"; *Points of Gold: Poems for Leo Luke Marcello*, ed. Stella Nesanovich (Xavier Review Press, 2005): "Sweet Olive"; *Prairie Schooner*: "I Don't Speak Lithuanian" (as "Aš Nekalbu Lietuviškai"), "Berry-Picking," "Bitch," and "Whisker"; *Valparaiso Poetry Review*: "Death of a Newsman" (as an untitled sonnet within the collaborative sonnet sequence titled "Frequencies").

The group of four poems published in *Prairie Schooner* received a 2007 Glenna Luschei Prairie Schooner Poetry Award.

"Used Book" won first place in the 2007 Open Poetry international sonnet competition and was reprinted in *Hand Luggage Only*, ed. Christopher Whitby (Open Poetry Ltd, 2008).

"Cold War Flashback," under the title "Hurricane Glass," received an honorable mention in the Boston University Alumni Poetry Competition.

"Whisker," "Bitch," "Player Piano," and "I Don't Speak Lithuanian" were published in Lithuanian translation in *Poezijos pavasaris '05*, ed. Valdas Kukulas and Laima Masytė (Vaga, 2005).

Special thanks to Cindy Kane and Ava Haymon for their advice in organizing this collection. Cecilia Loos, thank you for your help in getting Ava's comments to me. Thanks, as well, to all those who provided feedback on early drafts of the manuscript or on individual poems: Nahla and William Beier, Clayton Delery, Aaron Edwards, Susan Hardin, Laurence Lieberman, Stephanie Masson, Frank Schicketanz, Dave Smith, and Mary Kay Waskom.

The author is also deeply grateful to the U.S. Department of State (Council on International Exchange of Scholars) and the Louisiana Division of the Arts for the grants which provided time and inspiration to write.

This book is for my sisters, Sue and Cindy, and their families:
Dale, Doug, Hat, Nick, Darcy, and Eric.

Contents

3: CUTTING THE BODY LOOSE

JAZZ FUNERAL

"I felt a Funeral, in my Brain . . ."
—Emily Dickinson (Poem 280)

"A typical [New Orleans] jazz funeral begins with a march by the family, friends, and a brass band from the home, funeral home, or church to the cemetery. Throughout the march, the band plays somber dirges, hymns. A change in the tenor of the ceremony takes place, after the deceased is either buried, or the hearse leaves the procession and members of the procession say their final good bye and they 'cut the body loose.' After this the music becomes more upbeat, often starting with a hymn or spiritual number played in a swinging fashion, then going into popular hot tunes."
—*Wikipedia*, "Jazz funeral"

1: THE MARCH TO THE GRAVEYARD

Whisker

Suddenly, this barb growing out of my chin,
as sharp as the quill on a porcupine:
the fault of a middle-aged shift in hormones,
that dot of the Other in the yin-yang sign.
It's springing up fast as a giant's beanstalk,
so rapidly I worry that my face,
cut open, might yield one mile-long hair
curled up like a spool of measuring tape.
Suppose I stopped cutting it back each morning,
relinquished my scissors, Sisyphe on strike:
would it twirl from my jaw like a catfish's whisker,
a kingbird's *vibrissa*, a bighorn sheep's spike,
a frayed piece of line from a fight-weary fish?
If I can't be a Bishop, could I be a witch?

Bitch

"Oh, get yourself a life," my mother snapped
because I'd said "poor thing" about the moth-
er dog that came around to nose the cat
food set outside for strays, its dangling ud-
ders all the flesh that wasn't crimped to bone
like pie dough to a pan, its fur in patch-
es: ringworm, or the mange. Three times I'd phoned
the pound, but always she'd outfoxed the catch-
ers, weakened as she was. My mother, pooped
from shopping Jackson Square for peacock feath-
er masks, sipped sherry in my living room
and lost her houseguest manners altogeth-
er: "Get yourself a life," is what she said,
but, listen: I'm alive and she's long dead.

Heads or Tails

The lights are blinding and it stinks of pee
inside this clinic where I've rushed the cat,
and now the duty vet is telling me
the heart is failing and one lung's collapsed.
It's possible the lung could re-inflate
if they could drain the fluid off, except
the breathing problem means they can't sedate
the cat to stab that siphon through her chest.
Choose not to hurt her, she won't live the night.
So what's my vote, as an American?
To give my freedom up without a fight,
To be a choiceless little kid again.
"All right," I say. A razor shaves the spot.
Before they break the skin, the cat's heart stops.

Ode on Grimalkin Urns

One's celadon, an Asian ginger jar;
one's metal, overwrought with cartoon cats
attacking balls of yarn—think "Hallmark card";
and Poubelle's in a cube of cheap white plas-
tic, chez Le Corbusier. Cat-ashes, lugged
more years than I'll admit from digs to digs:
I'm running out of coffin-room to tuck them
under my toga like Plath's coiled kids.
My ex's mother had a poodle die
in Sabine, Texas, and her husband dug
its grave while she was sleeping, then forgot
precisely where in all that oilfield muck
he'd planted Happy. Heraclitus said:
Throw out like dung the bodies of the dead.

Player Piano

"Common as dirt, the TVs of their time,"
the used piano man in Boston sniffs
at my grandmother's twenties player piano
as I itemize the house, executrix;
insulting the Kane family heirloom that
I thought would make us rich, its wood veneer
now black as the mold on Irish potatoes
that brought all our sorry forebears here
to work in factories or drive a team,
on holidays to sing and get besotted
around the piano my grandmother bought,
its flap valves and leather bellows rotted,
but still, amazingly, in tune—one key
gone soundless as, at the appraisal, me.

Berry-Picking

Not knowing we'd be picking berries on
the ranch my friend was losing to divorce
the day I came to help her pack her stuff,
I'd put on sandals and a pair of shorts.
My friend, in jeans and sneakers, had to do
some rote-like thing to get her mind off loss,
and I can still remember glancing down
to see the zigzag red embroidery floss
of bramble-scratches stitched across my legs,
my ankles purple from the berry-juice,
a small adhesive bandage on one thigh
where I'd just had a berry-mole removed,
not knowing carefree days were at an end
for me as well as my divorcing friend.

Palanga Beach

Two summers after melanoma took
a "shark bite" from my right leg's upper thigh,
I'm brave enough to wear a bathing suit
in someone else's country, where men's eyes
lock automatically on native girls,
their hipless silhouettes, their high-heeled stride
while barefoot; so it's only the small kids
who stare at the pink slug four inches wide,
the ice cream scoop when I'm in profile. One
year afterward (an intermediate step),
I went to bed with an old boyfriend who
had loved me mainly for my long, white legs:
"Well, hell, looks better than a dead leg," he
assured me (wishing I were undersea).

I Don't Speak Lithuanian

To move to another country and not speak the language,
unable to tell where words start and end
in that river of speech-sounds, except when your name
is spoken, or *cake,* or some number one to ten,
is to be reborn as a one-year-old child
or a dog in the corner, its paws on its snout,
an astronaut drifting through galaxy static,
or blind Helen Keller, her hand in the spout.
Like that time in your childhood when millions of ladybugs
covered your swing-set, the sides of your house,
events appear to be conjured by magic
when you don't have the language to ask *why* or *how,*
so that you almost dread the day some chatter
locks, like a virus, to ports in gray matter.

The Great Man

"The man I'm going to introduce you to,
who taught so many of the poets here
this evening in his more than forty years
in Kaunas at Vytautas Magnus U.,
was on the front lines, one of very few
among us, when the Russian tanks appeared
to crush the rebels, who had commandeered
the TV station—Come, I'll speak for you."
The great man smiles at me: American,
still pretty, I suppose, in tavern-light.
I smile at him: a weathered tree, his white
beard turning into spirit at its ends.
Without a common tongue, we smile and stare
like children; then he bends to kiss my hair.

Cold War Flashback

IN MEMORIAM, ŠIAURYS NARBUTAS (1956–2008)

They led you away at dawn,
I followed you, like a mourner . . .
On your lips was the icon's chill.
—Anna Ahkmatova, "Requiem"

The hostess gifts you brought me were a joke:
a photograph of Lenin in a small red star
to pin to my lapel, assorted postcards
featuring the worst in Soviet art:
factories, tractors. We laughed so hard
we hiccupped. Later that night we passed
the kitschy gift shops on Bourbon Street.
I bought you a souvenir hurricane glass.
Then you were gone, and my morning paper
lay on the stoop in its cellophane bag,
as if not bringing it in could alter
news of the movements of Soviet tanks.
I blinked back tears at the Lenin pin.
I kissed that icon as the tanks rolled in.

Cardinal

This time last winter I abandoned you
or, rather, left you in the hands of God
and college kids demolishing my house
while I was teaching poetry abroad.
My last day home you came to feed at dusk,
your habit, bird of shadows, too exposed
in undiluted sunlight, malformed wing
draped rakishly as a dandy's cloak.
And though, back home again, I look for you,
I know deep down that was the final time.
What else was I to do? Not go? Take you?
To cage a songbird is a federal crime.
The yard is full of birds whose wings are whole,
but imperfection singled out your soul.

Mockingbird

That mockingbird could make me paranoid,
the way he's always got his eyes on me
(as if he were a cop in unmarked car)
from hidden stakeouts in the dogwood tree.
He wants to be the first to grab the chunks
of desiccated fruit from millet seeds;
like Pavlov's dog inside a feather-suit,
he's learned that I appear before he feeds.
I wonder, does he ever take a break,
relax his vigil, watch the butterflies?
Some nights I wake and shudder in my bed,
imagining those fixed, unblinking eyes,
or flash back suddenly to 21,
a pretty girl in crosshairs of a gun.

15 March 2003

"Beware the Ides of March," a seer said
to Caesar, back when death was hand-to-hand.
This year, two hundred thousand U.S. troops
camped on Kuwaiti and Saudi sand,
each with a dog tag tucked in a boot
and a belt-packed, camouflage poncho/shroud;
and still you breathe the fluid in and out,
preparing to breathe air just months from now.
No blood relation—though you grow inside
my sister's womb, and she and I share genes—
as much the product of technology
as laser-guided bombs and M16s,
you pull us toward the future, unborn niece,
as small and fragile as the hope of peace.

The Killing Field

A tell-tale pile of feathers in the yard
this morning, tip-off to a murder scene:
as if some nut had slit a pillowcase
or down-filled parka bought from L. L. Bean.
Detective work reveals the down is gray,
the longer feathers barred in gray and white,
which means the victim was a mockingbird,
the only bird that likes to sing at night;
like yelling "Here I am!" to thugs with guns.
By noon the criminal has been ID'd,
the tom I feed too full to come around
for day-old chow my two cats didn't eat.
Can't read the paper (nothing but the war)
or hold back moral judgment any more.

2: THE EULOGY

A Hobo's Crown for Robert Borsodi

(1939–2003)

Raised by his grandfather, the Depression-era philosopher Ralph Borsodi, Robert Borsodi graduated from Choate and the Yale University School of Drama, then turned his back on his privileged background. He opened a string of Beatnik-style coffeehouses throughout the American West, walking out on each one when the urge to wander struck him. He arrived in New Orleans in the 1970s and more or less stayed, although he shut down his coffeehouse to hop freight trains every summer and moved its uptown location three times before settling in a former crack house on Soniat Street. He continued to write, produce, direct, and act in plays for the benefit of his coffeehouse patrons; during the 1980s, he took his ragtag troupe to New York City several times and enjoyed brief runs off-off-Broadway. Terminally ill with bone cancer and lacking health insurance, he committed suicide by jumping from the Hale Boggs Bridge into the Mississippi River on October 25, 2003.

I.

Warm as a campfire on a bitter night:
that was your vision of a coffeehouse,
so, even though they were passé back then,
you set up shop and hung your shingle out
and gave bohemians a place to go
like Frisco in the fifties: bongo drums
and cool cat daddios and felt berets
tipped rakishly on brows of Dharma bums.
Who would have guessed that, twenty years ahead,
we'd find one popping up on every block,
a mocha latte filling every mug,
if not the chicken gracing every pot
once promised by a Dust Bowl populist
in times that fit you, that you somehow missed.

2.

In times that fit you, that you somehow missed,
your father's father, Ralph Borsodi, built
two model self-sufficient villages
among the Great Depression's Hoovervilles;
wrote treatises on canning, weaving clothes,
the upper-limit size of neighborhoods.
They say he raised you, when your parents split,
to shun big business and consumer goods,
which might explain why you would never shop
in stores (preferring curbside garbage cans),
or take a razor to your waist-long beard,
or stand in judgment of your fellow man,
although, at night, inside your coffee shop,
you heard the guns of urban rage go off.

3.

You heard the guns of urban rage go off,
but Nancy, in the shower, heard a CRACK!
and felt an object whack her in the head
the week you left us, worrying you'd laugh
to greet Anubis in the Hall of Truth,
a feather trembling in his weighing-cup,
and make him angry at your lack of faith
in anything but too, too solid stuff.
But back to Nancy, worried for your soul:
she found a piece of plastic by the drain,
no bigger than a Harrah's poker chip,
not broken off from fan or ceiling paint,
and guessed you meant to tell her she was right
about the jackal-god and afterlife.

4.

About the jackal-god and afterlife
you didn't worry, having lots of time,
unlike the patrons of the coffeehouse
who watched your beard grow as they stood in line—
the new ones, college kids or tourists armed
with guidebooks claiming that the place was cool,
who wondered how the words "Mu tea" could take
eight minutes to propel you off your stool
to pour hot water in an ancient cup.
Well, hell: they had the parrot overhead
for entertainment. Parrot-keepers know
that chances are they'll be the first one dead.
Your deathlike silence made my tongue go slack.
I'd blush bright crimson when you stared me back.

5.

I'd blush bright crimson when you stared me back:
no veiling secrets with a redhead's skin.
My surgeon said the melanoma wards
were full of victims who could be my twin,
"My people!" as the Ugly Duckling cried
on glimpsing snowy plumage through the reeds,
or Sherlock's carrot-crested villain thought
on seeing posters for the Redheaded League.
Your beard was reddish, but your tumor bone;
your cancer hidden, as my own was plain;
your odds were zero, mine were two in three;
so many of us gone, who signed our names
each New Year's Day inside your ledger-book
and ate your black-eyed peas to bring us luck.

6.

We ate your black-eyed peas to bring us luck,
your slimy cabbage, and the lumps of dough
you called "croissants," but which resembled, more,
the kind of biscuits kept on hand to throw
to man's best friend for shaking the right paw
or begging. Beggars can't be choosers, though:
the food was free, the poets out in force
from uptown mansions and downtown skid row.
And meanwhile, on a hundred other blocks
with windows made of glass, not plywood boards,
PJ's and Starbuck's and Rue de la Course
rang up sales of peppermint and eggnog
holiday coffees, muffins big as heads,
bombarding every sense to steal our bread.

7.

Bombarding every sense to steal our bread,
your rivals focused on the bottom line,
while you got by and even bought the house
your shop was in with coffee-can-chunked dime
and nickel tips. You never told
a soul your pedigree was Choate and Yale,
filled applications out left-handed so
they'd take your dungarees and ponytail
for working class and not New Haven chic.
From time to time you worked construction jobs
between the walked-away-from coffee shops—
eleven in as many cities, Bob,
all named "Borsodi's," in your one salute
to patriarchy and the men in suits.

8.

To patriarchy and the men in suits
I might have toasted when I met a tax
attorney in Borsodi's coffeehouse
who'd snuck in brandy in a silver flask
back then when anything could happen, when
the yarrow stalks were rolling hexagrams.
The tax attorney liked my poetry
or legs, and pulled a piece of marzipan
from one vest-pocket of his pinstriped suit
as, later, on his patchwork leather couch,
he'd tend to business like I wasn't there
and liquidate the surplus in accounts—
one scene of many from those crazy days
when we were players on Borsodi's stage.

9.

When we were players on Borsodi's stage,
our undisputed star was Sara Beth.
I saw her tap-dance in a hammock once,
jump in and out and never miss a step;
and once, in U.S. Army camouflage,
a plastic rifle in her doll-sized hands,
she sounded like a whole damn regiment
with Janet Jackson still in training pants.
I saw her, after you and she broke up,
performing for a crowd on Bourbon Street,
fat tourists throwing quarters as she tapped;
then Gary told me she had burned her feet
and needed money, and I wrote a check.
She wasn't in the write-up on your death.

10.

She wasn't in the write-up on your death,
but every summer you and she would lock
the coffeehouse and pack a few effects
to carry with you as you freight-train-hopped
to points out west where hoboes weren't extinct.
Who says you can't repeat a country's past?
You rode the rails to 1933,
where good faced evil over iron tracks.
Around the time the first Gulf War played out
on television like a game of Pong,
or maybe after Father Karl got shot
for pocket money as he walked his dog,
you gave it up for good, did not leave town,
lost track of who had won the hobo's crown.

11.

Lost track of who had won the hobo's crown,
that quaint Depression custom. You can bet,
these days, Reality TV would jump
to have the homeless court The Bachelorette
or seek apprenticeship to Donald Trump
by farting loudest after eating beans
or roasting rodents over Sterno cans
while chugging rotgut out of tin canteens.
They'd move the contest to a tropic isle
and slap up dummy trains and railroad tracks,
then bring in *Queer Eye*'s crew to renovate
bandanna pouches into Gucci sacks. . .
One thing we had in common, you and I:
pop culture was a train that passed us by.

12.

Pop culture was a train that passed us by
on tracks like those near the suspension bridge
from Destrehan to Luling, swamp to swamp,
on which they found your empty car, igni-
tion off; and Nancy said you might have hopped
a freight train, made it look as if you'd jumped;
you might be starting up a new Borsodi's
somewhere yet un-Disneyed and un-Trumped.
And when they couldn't find your body, I
kept hoping she was right, it wasn't real:
the divers dredging in the muddy river
under that stretch of rust-colored steel
that could have been designed by Frank Lloyd Wright
to look like part of nature on its site.

13.

To look like part of nature on its site—
a playwright's backdrop, while the divers searched
and Jimmy told us how you tried to see
a doctor when the pain kept getting worse,
but sat for days on end in Charity,
Art Deco palace for the dying poor,
while no one called your name, until you said
"the hell with it" and beat it out the door,
below carved figures that the government
bequeathed to us as anodyne for pain
when artists drew a paycheck from the state
and bullets hadn't ended Long's campaign,
then drove your flowered truck from friend to friend
to beg for help in bringing on the end.

14.

To beg for help in bringing on the end:
who wants to dwell on things like that when fate
lets up the pressure, lets us sit with friends
on common ground awhile and celebrate
what binds us to each other and a place
despite that whistle urging us to run,
despite the knowledge that a levee break
could level it like a one-megaton
atomic blast? You never lived to see
the halls of Charity entombed with mold,
dead bodies strewn like roadkill in the streets,
Borsodi's flooded like a toilet bowl.
Thank God for that, at least. We miss your light,
warm as a campfire on a bitter night.

3: CUTTING THE BODY LOOSE

First Re-Entry, Post-Katrina

As if a friend you used to see a lot
but haven't, lately, stops you on the street,
and right away you note the baseball cap,
the skeleton that has begun to peek
through facial features, and you hear about
the son or daughter in from out of town,
the chemo up at Willis twice a week,
how hard it is to keep a milkshake down:
The City Care Forgot (and then recalled)
comes into focus from your moving car,
whole blocks of houses with their doors kicked in
and rooflines covered with blue FEMA tarps,
and though prognostication's inexact
you see yourself which way the odds are stacked.

The Terror of the Place

Like Juliet reviving in the tomb,
you blink and blink and still your eyes behold
the walls of what was once a music room
grown over with great roses of black mold,
the grand piano caving in on shat-
tered legs as if a camel knelt to let
a tourist with a camera on its back.
Disaster tourist—is that you? You step
on sodden books and papers inches deep,
a stuck-together pulp. Like ancient Rome,
the pottery is all that's left to keep—
a bust, a vase—from what was once a home.
So early waking—what with loathsome smells . . .
Escaping death, you find yourself in hell.

Those Sunday Drives

You used to bore me with your monologues
on drives through old "New Awlins" neighborhoods:
what family had what house when you were young
and where some candy store or bank had stood.
Who cares about the past? I used to think.
We Yankee Irish pulled up roots a lot,
escaping relatives with chicken coops
and cabbage boiling in a kitchen pot.
But that was all before the hurricane
our Mason-Dixon love did not survive—
a minor loss beside the numbered dead,
four houses flooded out of every five.
So much has changed. Time speeded up her clock,
And now I bore all riders with my talk.

Death of a Newsman

IN MEMORIAM, EDWIN JULIAN KANE (1924–2000)

The night sky is bright with the grieving Pleiades,
rising in the season your voice was stilled at last,
though sound itself never dies, your every newscast
spiraling out through space to distant galaxies.
When I was little, I thought you knelt in TVs.
I walked around them looking for a door and latch.
Heads jerked in swordfish-netted restaurants when you asked
for a menu. Women sent you cold remedies.
News of the ancient gods precedes your voice through space,
bulletins about rapists and transformations,
sisters scattered to stars, riding on waves of sound;
briefly, your news of protests, assassinations;
then, in the wake of your inimitable bass,
towers struck and destroyed, a much-loved city drowned.

Sweet Olive

IN MEMORIAM, LEO LUKE MARCELLO (1945–2005)

Sweet olive, blooming when the weather shifts
from shorts to winter coats, or coats to shorts;
for centuries before conditioned air,
planted just outside the kitchen door
to swish that otherworldly odor through
the screen-holes, maddening the young and old
with something hard to put a finger on,
as dangerous as powder up the nose . . .
Small tree of knowledge, pulling victims off
the sidewalk tracking your elusive smell,
past sun-struck lizards or the birdbath's ice,
to linger here for decades in its spell:
Why can't we leave your native South behind?
What grows here grows from the unconscious mind.

Hermit Crabs

Like someone kicked you in the stomach, when
you saw a heap of them for sale beside
a bin of flip-flops at Rehoboth Beach,
wheeling your dad around before he died.
Painted in psychedelic colors, doves
& flags & peace signs—why the sixties theme?
The way some lunatics will paint their homes
in gold & purple for a football team.
Creatures are made to suffer every day,
baby seals clubbed and kittens drowned in sacks—
so what was it about those hermit crabs
that made you fantasize you'd buy them back
and free them under moonlight, at low tide,
to choose a prison cell to crawl inside?

Not Another Elegy for You

You must have had a thousand writer-friends,
so, when your heart gave out before its time,
they wrote about your grace at poetry
and basketball, your love of jazz and wine.
But not one elegy has told the truth
about your body odor—how you stunk.
Nineteen, your student, sitting next to you,
I breathed that pepper-incense, getting drunk
on possibilities of words and flesh.
Two decades later, you forgot to pack
a ratty sweater when you left my house.
I sniffed and sniffed it till I mailed it back.
Did you not bathe, or were your glands at fault?
The human stink gets purged inside the vault.

Rising and Falling

Why not say "falling *out* of love," the truth,
and "rising *into* love," like other things—
soap bubbles, dust motes, helium balloons,
and bird or Icarus or insect wings—
that yank the stupid kite strings of the heart
by catching giddy updrafts while they last
before they plummet back where all flights start
in a smooth landing or a fatal crash?
It's true: one time I logged eleven years
of soaring thermal currents fancy-free
before I saw the telltale signs appear
that meant *he'd* fallen out of love with *me*.
Don't trust the crap you read about in rhyme:
Gravity will win out every time.

Particle Physics

They say two photons fired through a slit
stay paired together to the end of time;
if one is polarized to change its spin,
the other does a U-turn on a dime,
although they fly apart at speeds of light
and never cross each other's paths again,
like us, a couple in the seventies,
divorced for almost thirty years since then.
Tonight a Red Sox batter homered twice
to beat the Yankees in their playoff match,
and, sure as I was born in Boston, when
that second ball deflected off the bat,
I knew your thoughts were flying back to me,
though your location was a mystery.

Finale

How you'd begin would never be the same;
at times you'd even face me for awhile.
But always, in that drive before you came,
you'd flip me over, finish doggy-style.
Another funny thing: you'd never try
to steal a peek at me when I undressed.
I wondered if you'd rather have a guy,
if that was why you covered up my breasts.
Or maybe I was wrong, and you were straight,
but ex or mama used to yak, yak, yak;
you'd shove my mouth into the pillowcase
to face an uncommunicative back.
I haven't met her yet, your newest friend,
and yet I'd bet my butt about the end.

Used Book

What luck—an open bookstore up ahead
as rain lashed awnings over Royal Street,
and then to find the books were secondhand,
with one whole wall assigned to poetry;
and then, as if that wasn't luck enough,
to find, between Jarrell and Weldon Kees,
the blue-on-cream, familiar backbone of
my chapbook, out of print since '83—
its cover very slightly coffee-stained,
but aging (all in all) no worse than flesh
through all those cycles of the seasons since
its publication by a London press.
Then, out of luck, I read the name inside:
The man I thought would love me till I died.

Purple Martin Suite

"I had several opportunities, at the period of their arrival, of seeing prodigious flocks moving over [New Orleans] or its vicinity, at a considerable height . . . I walked under one of them with ease for upwards of two miles, at that rate on the 4th of February 1821, on the bank of the river below the city, constantly looking up at the birds, to the great astonishment of many passengers, who were bent on far different pursuits."
—John James Audubon

I.

Any excuse, a holiday or death
will make them twirl umbrellas, shake their butts
to brass band music in the streets. I swear,
what *won't* these people make a party of?
So when my neighbor loaded beer on ice
and grabbed two folding chairs and said he meant
to go watch birds roost underneath a bridge,
it seemed no odder an excuse than Lent
to celebrate. We parked the pickup truck
by Entergy and slid down dirt banks under
girders where the Causeway Bridge meets land,
silenced by the rush-hour traffic's thunder
whizzing overhead. No sign, yet, of a bird:
I had to take my neighbor at his word.

2.

I had to take my neighbor at his word
that there would be a show, as birds arrived
in ones and twos and then in blue-black streams
from day locations up to thirty miles
in all directions, by my neighbor's math.
This was the staging ground for their migration
southward, down the Gulf of Mexico,
to the far corners of the Amazon Basin:
bridgeworks to rest on and clouds of mosquitoes
ripe for the sunset-plucking on this lake
where no one sane would build a city (floods
& yellow fever), let alone then take
the scraps left over and build backyard homes
for birds that can't build shelters on their own.

3.

For birds that can't build shelters on their own
we'd gathered, half a dozen of us there.
At first the martins flew at random, making
meaningless blue-black scribbles on the air,
thousands and thousands of them swarming; then,
as if an orchestra were tuning up,
the sun dipped under the horizon like
the fall of a baton, the "theater" hushed,
and suddenly the birds began to soar
in perfect loop-de-loops and barrel rolls,
whole squadrons of them flying synchronized
as vintage prop planes in an aircraft show,
till even those not mystically inclined
would swear they were connected mind to mind.

4.

As if they were connected mind to mind,
one group of them broke off and swooped en masse
below the Causeway, settling wing to wing
along steel girders; then a second pass,
a third, as any birds who hadn't found
a spot the last dive, flowed into the next,
the way a mother braids a daughter's hair
or villanelle picks up old lines of text.
When they were finished it was way too dark
to tell their outlines from the sky or lake.
We stood and clapped as if we'd seen the Meters
reunited on a Jazz Fest stage,
joined beat to beat and holding in our breath
as night fell on that holiday from death.

Notes

"Whisker": "Bishop" refers to Elizabeth Bishop, whose famous image from "The Fish" has been stolen in the preceding line.

"Ode on Grimalkin Urns": This time, the stolen image (of two dead children coiled at the dead mother's breasts) is from Sylvia Plath's "Edge."

"Palanga Beach": Palanga Beach is located on the Baltic Coast of Lithuania.

"The Great Man" and **"Cold War Flashback"**: These poems refer to the incident of January 13, 1991, in Vilnius, Lithuania, when Russian tanks and troops closed in on Lithuanian rebels holed up in the city's TV tower, killing twelve Lithuanians.

"A Hobo's Crown for Robert Borsodi": Cast of characters in this crown of sonnets (also called a "corona"): "Nancy" is Nancy Harris; "Sara Beth" is Sara Beth Peters; "Gary" is Gary Talarchek; "Father Karl" is the Reverend Karl Petersen, slain in New Orleans in 1995 near his Church of St. Peter and Paul in Faubourg Marigny; and "Jimmy" is Jimmy Ross. "Harrah's," in poem 3, is a New Orleans casino; "Charity," in poem 13, is Charity Hospital in New Orleans; and "Long" is Louisiana governor and U.S. presidential hopeful Huey Long, who was assassinated in the Baton Rouge State Capitol in 1935.

"First Re-Entry, Post-Katrina": "Willis" is the Willis Knighton Cancer Center in Shreveport, Louisiana.

"The Terror of the Place": The title and penultimate line are taken from Shakespeare's *Romeo and Juliet.*

"Death of a Newsman": This was the writer's individual contribution to a seven-poem crown of sonnets written by seven women poets. The first line of this poem was the last line of a sonnet by Judith Barrington, and the last line of this poem became the first line of a sonnet by Kathrine Varnes.

"Particle Physics": The baseball game in question was the seventh game of the 2004 American League playoffs between the Boston Red Sox and the New York Yankees, in Yankee Stadium. Red Sox player Johnny Damon hit two home runs, including a grand slam.

"Purple Martin Suite": The epigraph is from John James Audubon's chapter titled "The Purple Martin" in his *Ornithological Biography* (1831). The 24-mile-long Causeway Bridge connects New Orleans with the north shore of Lake Pontchartrain. At its south end, the bridge provides a roost and staging ground for approximately two hundred thousand purple martins on their annual fall migration to South America.

Biographical Note

Julie Kane is a past National Poetry Series winner, Fulbright Scholar, and Louisiana Poet Laureate. Coeditor with Grace Bauer of *Nasty Women Poets: An Unapologetic Anthology of Subversive Verse*, she has published five books and two chapbooks of poetry as well as nonfiction and translations. Her work can be found in over sixty anthologies, including Penguin's *Pocket Poetry*, Norton's *Seagull Reader*, and *Best American Poetry 2016*. She lives in Natchitoches, Louisiana, and teaches in the low-residency MFA program at Western Colorado University.

Printed in the USA
CPSIA information can be obtained
at www.ICGtesting.com
JSHW081353080124
54999JS00002B/238